WHAT IF YOU HAD

Animal Hair!?

by Sandra Markle

Illustrated by
Howard McWilliam

Scholastic Inc.

With love for
Piper Rose Jeffery

Text copyright © 2014 by Sandra Markle
Illustrations copyright © 2014 by Howard McWilliam

All rights reserved. Published by Scholastic Inc. SCHOLASTIC and associated logos are trademarks and/or registered trademarks of Scholastic Inc.

ISBN 978-0-545-63085-6

14 13 12 11 10   14 15 16 17 18 19/0

Printed in the U.S.A.   40
First printing, January 2014
Art direction by Paul W. Banks
Design by Kay Petronio

What if one day when you woke up, the hair on your head wasn't yours? What if, overnight, a wild animal's hair grew in, instead?

polar bear

A polar bear has a double coat of hair to keep it warm. There's a woolly undercoat close to the bear's skin. Above that is a top coat made of six-inch-long, stiff, oil-coated hairs. A polar bear's hair looks as white as Arctic snow because the top-coat hairs are hollow and clear. They reflect the light just like snow!

fact

Each May or June, a polar bear sheds its hair and grows a whole new coat in less than a month.

If you had polar bear hair on your head, you could play outdoors in cold, wet weather and never need a hat.

5

Reindeer

A reindeer has a double coat, too. It also has a lot of hair—as many as 5,000 outer hairs per square inch of skin. Each long, stiff outer hair has a hollow core. These hairs trap air. In addition to keeping the reindeer warm, its hair helps this heavy animal float in the water.

Fact

A reindeer's hollow hairs keep its body heat from escaping. In fact, if a reindeer lies on the ground, the snow under it doesn't melt.

If you had reindeer hair, swimming would always be easy, even in the roughest of waters.

MUSK OX

A musk ox has the longest hair of any wild animal. Some hairs are as long as two feet! Its shaggy coat hangs down to its hooves. This coat is also double thick and so tough it acts like a suit of armor.

fact

Each spring, a musk ox sheds its woolly undercoat—as much as seven pounds of hair.

If you had musk ox hair, you could play outside day or night, in winter or summer, without worrying about frostbite, sunburn, or bug bites.

9

oryx

A scimitar-horned oryx has hair that is just right for its African desert home. The oryx's pale-colored coat reflects sunlight and keeps it from overheating. The hairs are also so short that any cool breezes easily reach its skin.

fact

Oryx calves are born with solid yellow coats. They develop distinctive markings and pale-white-and-red coats as they grow up.

If you had scimitar-horned oryx hair, you'd never need a comb or a brush. Even if you rolled on the ground, your hair would be too short to tangle or collect dirt.

Lion

A male lion has a mane—long, thick hair on the back of its head, neck, and shoulders. When it comes to having a mane, size matters. Scientists learned that female lions, called lionesses, prefer males with big manes. That could be because the healthiest males usually have the largest manes.

fact

A lion's mane needs regular cleaning and grooming. Luckily, a group of lions, called a pride, will groom one another. These big cats have a built-in comb—their rough tongues.

If you had a lion's mane, you'd stand out in a crowd. You'd look big and bold.

13

zebra

A zebra's hair grows in black and white stripes. These stripes help it stay safe. Whether standing still or running, zebras usually stick together in a herd. Seeing so many stripes confuses hunters such as lions and hyenas.

fact

A zebra's hair shows if it's healthy or sick. The short hair on a healthy zebra's mane stands up straight. A sick zebra's mane flops over to the side.

If you had zebra hair, you wouldn't have to work at being one of a kind. Each zebra has a stripe pattern that is completely unique.

15

three-toed sloth

A three-toed sloth's hair often looks green because little plants, called algae, grow all over it. Sloths live in damp rain forests and rarely move, making their bodies a good place for algae to live. However, having green hair isn't a bad thing. Green hair helps sloths blend into their homes in the treetops and hide from predators such as jaguars and harpy eagles.

fact

Three-toed sloths spend most of their lives upside down, so their hair grows differently than other hairy animals. When a three-toed sloth hangs upside down, its hair falls over its body. So even upside down, the sloth's hair keeps its skin dry when it rains.

If you had three-toed sloth hair, you'd never be alone. Because of the algae, your hair would be home to many different kinds of harmless insects.

Arctic Fox

An Arctic fox's hair is snow-white in winter. Each hair is also fat, helping make its coat thick and warm. As the days grow longer and heat up, an Arctic fox sheds its wintertime hair and grows a new brown coat. Now each hair is skinny, helping make its coat thin and keeping the fox from overheating. Besides staying comfortable, changing its coat keeps an Arctic fox perfectly colored to sneak up on prey such as lemmings and voles.

fact

When getting ready for winter, Arctic foxes also grow long hair between their toes and on the soles of their feet. Their furry feet help them run on ice without slipping.

If you had Arctic fox hair, you'd never get tired of your hair color because it would change with the seasons.

giant pangolin

A giant pangolin's body is covered with scales, which consist of the same substance as hair. Like hair, the scales are made of tough keratin and grow out of the skin. A giant pangolin's scales also start small and grow longer until, at last, they fall out. New scales grow in to replace the ones that are lost.

fact

The back edges of a giant pangolin's scalelike hairs are razor-sharp. So if it's attacked, a giant pangolin just curls up tight to stay safe.

If you had a giant pangolin's scales, you wouldn't need to put on a helmet to ride your bike.

21

porcupine

A porcupine has a normal coat but it also has special hairs, too, called quills. Quills are stiff, needlelike hairs. If attacked, barbs on the end of each quill poke into the enemy's skin. Then even when they separate, the porcupine's quills stay stuck in the enemy.

fact

A porcupine's skin gives off a fatty substance that coats each quill. This fatty substance contains a germ-killing chemical. So if a porcupine accidentally pokes itself, it won't get an infection.

If you had a porcupine's quills, bullies would never bother you.

star-nosed mole

A star-nosed mole's hair, unlike most animal hair, can lie flat in any direction. Pushed forward, sideways, or straight back, its hair will never stick up. It will always lie flat against its body. This lets a star-nosed mole slip easily through its underground tunnels whether it's going forward or backing up.

fact

A star-nosed mole has comblike claws to spread oil through its hair. That makes its coat waterproof. That's important since it lives in damp tunnels.

If you had star-nosed mole hair, your hair would stay put whatever direction you comb it.

Wild-animal hair could be cool for a while. But you don't use your hair to stay afloat or confuse predators. You don't need your hair to change with the seasons, be a helmet, or lie flat in every direction.

And you'll never defend yourself with your hair—no matter what.
So if you could keep wild-animal hair for more than a day, which kind would be right for you?

Luckily, you don't have to choose.

The hair that grows on top of your head may look wild from time to time, but it will always be people hair.

It will be what you need to protect your head from heat, chills, and bumps; and make you look your best when it's clean and brushed.

HOW DOES HAIR GROW?

Hair growth starts in the root. The root is a cluster of cells, living building blocks, inside a tiny, saclike hole in the skin, called the *hair follicle*. This cluster of cells produces layer after layer of new hair cells. As these layers build up, the old dead cells—making up the *hair shaft*—are pushed out of the skin. As long as the root is alive, a hair on your head will continue to grow at a rate of about five inches a year, up to a maximum of about three feet.

Check out one of your hairs by gently pulling it free. Don't worry about losing this hair. Every day, you naturally lose as many as one hundred hairs. Then each old hair that is lost is replaced by a new one.

Take a close look at a single hair's shaft with a magnifying glass. The shape determines whether, as the hair grows, it's straight, wavy, or curly. Straight hair has a round shaft, wavy hair has an oval shaft, and curly hair has a flat shaft.

HOW DO YOU TAKE care of your hair?

The best way to keep your hair healthy and growing well is to eat right. Healthy hair needs a diet that includes protein from meat, fish, milk, cheese, beans, nuts, or eggs. It also needs vitamin B from foods including yogurt and whole grains, and iron, copper, and iodine from foods such as shellfish and leafy green vegetables.

It's important to clean hair regularly. Wild animals spend a lot of time and effort caring for their hair. Many animals—cats, for example—lick their fur to wash and comb it. Some animals that live in groups, such as monkeys, help each other care for their hair.

The most important thing to remember is that hair is part of your body. As long as you take good care of yourself, your hair will stay healthy.